The Ward

by

Louisa Campbell

The Ward

First published in Great Britain in 2018
by Paper Swans Press

ISBN 978-1-9998196-4-4

paperswans.co.uk
editor@paperswans.co.uk

Contents

To Doris, Gabriel, Tina, Ted, Bill, Jean and the rest of us.

Room 1

It was just before dawn when she
stopped.
Middle lane of the M25.
Unclunked her seatbelt, opened the door,
got out, walked barefoot
to the front of her Ford
and stood.
Gazing ahead, not seeing
lorries swerve past; not feeling
the backdrafts ruffle her hair;
not hearing horns blasting.

A van driver brought her in;
she was lucky.
We must find her some slippers.
She works in a shop. No kids.
There's an uncle somewhere;
we'll try to locate him.

Still, in her hospital nightie,
stuck in that spot
at the foot of her bed,
staring ...

Say? She says only one phrase
(makes you jump when she speaks):

I have seen myself.

Yes, that's it – nothing more –
and goes on staring.

Sussel

They comes up atwixt the bricks
into my cottage.
Chance-born, breachy, anywhen.
Creep behind me,
follow my creak,
slide past my slam.
Certain sure they slip their brandirons
into my sieving head,
chacket out brabagious words,
whip my mind aslew,
catercross, addled.

Oh, you're a footy one
'n' always vlothered;
maunderin' like a galleybird –
nunty, niff, gnang.
No need to get all tiffy
in that swollocky old head of yours;
chance-born we may be,
but at least we b'ain't insane.

Aslew: Aslant
Anywhen: At any time
Brabagious: Quarrelsome, an adjective of reproach
Brandirons: Irons used for supporting the brands for burning wood in a wood fire
Breachy: Wild and, applied to cattle, able to break through fences
Chance-born: Illegitimate
Chacket: Cough
Brabagious: Quarrelsome, an adjective of reproach
Catercross: Slanting

Footy: Silly, foolish, worthless
Galleybird: Woodpecker
Gnang: To gnash the teeth
Maundering: Mutter or grumble
Niff: Quarrel, be offended
Nunty: Sulky
Sussel: Disturbance, impertinent meddling in the affairs of other people
Swallocky: The appearance of clouds before a storm
Tiffy: Touchy, irritable
Timmersome: Timid
Vlothered: Agitated, flustered

From *A Dictionary of the Sussex Dialect*

Accept the Diagnosis

Ira Lightman and Louisa Campbell

Take me in your arms

Take me in to you in me

my darling disease

dada darling diregnosease

stitch your soft lips

stitch it itch soft softly mouth

to my gaping mouth

to my lyre liar lips

lock your sweet gaze

lock locked sweetie sweeter gaze

on my aching eyes

on my I-yes eyers ache

and whisper that I must

wispy whisper musky must

love you, love you.

love-a-bella love-a-label lover love you

The Ward

It's not the jump-proof windows,
collapsible, noose-defying hinges
or the glint of the hook-shaped ligature-cutter
in matron's locked cupboard.

It's not the shake of the ward clerk's small hand
as she picks up the 'phone,
the doctor's careful avoidance of eye contact,
nurses' cheery smiles.

It's not the little lock of grey hair
in the corner of the non-slip floor,
or the amber stains
on the wipe-clean duvet.

It's not the scent of *Dettol* mingling with
lunch-time's fried fish,
rattle of the drug trolley, thud
of the filing cabinet drawer.

It's not even the chain on the hospital teaspoon
in the patients' wary kitchen.

It's the long white corridor that carries you

from

nothing

to

nowhere.

Taxi Taxi

Taxi taxi slinky eye seek souls.
Taxi taxi circles, taxi swish
quiet, quiet taxi tyres,
taxi taxi engine hushful creep.

Taxi taxi slam black shut.
Taxi taxi see your thoughts,
count them up in taxi meter.
Taxi taxi swallow gulp.

I've seen driver lick his fingers,
I've seen victim stagger after;
stumble out on pavement stunned,
blink, sick, hollow.

All at Sea

His mood floats silently, steel in dark water:
a sea mine, ancient, but ready to blow.

Baccy-stained fingers grip empty green cup
while he steadily sways, as if with the waves.

Sometimes, in the depths of the navy-blue night
he flounders; his limbs start to twitch and tread water.

His memories; tendrils, cut off, but still wriggling.
Thoughts clang like a warning bell far from the shore;

one day his voice will come in with the tide,
writhing with squid from the clutter of ocean

or rising in inky-dark bubbles with kraken:
I want to come up now, bloop-bloop, bloop-bloop.

ECT Suite

l.

No one ever tells you why in 1937 the famous neurologist Ugo Cerletti didn't wait in the butcher's shop; he strolled round the back to the abattoir and watched pigs being anaesthetised with electroshock. He believed seizures were therapeutic. Sometimes they are, but no one knows why. We can deduce, however, that Ugo Cerletti liked bacon.

ll.

The ECT suite is decorated in a soft jade green, to induce calm. It has a kitchenette, toilets with wash hand basins, a recovery room and a treatment room. The ECT machine is about the size of a toaster. It's finished in a jaunty powder blue, but when you look at it, you still think *Frankenstein.*

lll.

Doris was 5 feet 2 inches and weighed seven stone. No one knows when she decided there was no point in eating, or when she last washed, or spoke. They gave her a leaflet which said no one knows how ECT works and that she wouldn't convulse, she would twitch, but no one knows whether she read it. They removed her dentures and the two metal hairgrips in her grey matted hair. They gave her an anaesthetic, a muscle relaxant, and a mouth guard to stop her biting her tongue. They placed padded electrodes on her temples, then administered about enough volts to power a lightbulb.

lV.

Three days later, Doris was cycling up Blackberry Hill on a pink bicycle to pick up her pension. She fancied a bacon butty.

Lollipop

It's pie-easy,
I look in the mirror and see the blubber;
cling of wobbling gloop.
The slosh of nausea
flops slug-like up my gullet,
curls my bile-taste tongue.

I won't set foot in McDonald's again.
Greggs can go screw themselves –
I can laugh in the face of a freshly-baked loaf,
stomp it to crumbs –
squish Haribo with my heel.

Now there's just me in my dry skull;
skin stretched over skeleton
like mother's picnic gazebo
on collapsible poles.

She says I look like a Chupa Chup.
She can say what she likes.

Accountant

When he started each morning roaring blood, he knew this was the beginning of his final audit. Years balancing other people's numbers. Symptoms accumulated; fiscal, visceral.

fear = unbearable
anger = acceptable
therefore, substitute fear for anger

Everyone at home, in the City, at the club knew. No one said a word or suggested lower alcohol by volume. They wrote him off.

He disbursed himself into empty Smirnoff bottles: 2 lying under the sofa; 3 on the mantelpiece; 93 in a stack outside the kitchen door, turning greeny-black.

whiskey = violent = problem
vodka = calm = no problem
therefore, vodka = no problem

The husk of him still moves with his winner's gait. Bloated face glares at the nurse, then requests, *If it's not too much trouble, could I possibly have my medication now?*

2 bottles daily = problem
4 x half bottles daily = half the problem
therefore half bottles = improvement

In the support group he says, *I apologise, but I have no problems to divulge* and sits, 1 of the circle of 12 people on plastic chairs, alone.

In the tai chi class, sweat gushes from him; collects in little lakes on the non-slip floor. He learns it is chi, working on his liver, expediting the detox. In Eastern medicine, it is understood that anger sits in the liver.

Which adds up.

For the psychiatrist who asks his patients whether they suffered their side effects before or after they'd seen the drug information leaflet

He must believe madness is catching;
seeps up his nostrils,
clings at the back of his throat.
He must be afraid of it budding inside him;
worried he'll wake with a judder, at midnight,
devoured by our lunacy,
howling.

Gabriel's Going

I told him he can take me soon.
Can you hear him?
Quiet, quiet, *shhh...*
He rings a crooked little bell.

Some families whizz down hills on bicycles,
legs out to the sides
feet waggling,
resting on gravity,
gravity, see?
Wheeee!
And ringing their bells; *ting ting!*

Some families go on holiday
in a big estate car.
They sing songs on the journey;
what do they sing?
Let us sing! Let us sing
All things Bright and Beautiful.

Beautiful Becky! I was lucky with Becky,
lucky Becky lucky Becky luck
before he came for me.
Me, I'm twenty-two.

I was lucky I went to Uni
before he came for me. Classics.
Blum blum blum bli blo blo bla bla bla!

Can you hear him? *Ting ting ting!*
I'm going now.
I won't talk to you
any more.

When the nurse read Mary Oliver's poem 'Wild Geese' to the patient

Somehow it skipped and slid into his mind
below tousled hair, behind glazed eyes;
made itself comfy on the scruffy sofa
next to the aliens, put its feet up
while the thought-ray bots
put the kettle on.

Maybe it was the pulse of the rhythm that held him,
or maybe, to him, the words had 'actions',
like rhymes from primary colour days
before he'd learned to keep watch.

Perhaps he just knew a good poem when he heard one,
or perhaps he needed to hear again and again
that he could have *a place in the family of things.*

But in that morning's ward round,
when he dropped to his joyful knees,
shuffled across to her, beaming,
Poem Nurse, Poem Nurse, say it with me!
She looked up from the glow of him
to the steel drug trolley,
doctor's wide eyes.

Asylum

These days, you can almost see tumbleweed
shambling round the ward.
Grey plastic hands on the clock can't be bothered;
point to whatever.
Sometimes you can work on the nurse
to take you up to the hospital shop,
but that only uses ten dull minutes
for vacuous *Wordsearch* and *Heat*.

Back then you took willow rods,
grown on trees by the lake on the farm;
the nurse would trust you with the
heavy steel bodkin to plait and
weave the spidery twigs;
a basket takes shape,
something good,
wholesome.

We'd walk from gardening *good-tired*,
mud in fingernails, giggling.
Who saw us

single
file
trail
through
the
'gate on its own'

sticking up from the grass like Ted's last bottom tooth might think we
were bonkers, not know we kept off the cricket pitch; hallowed green
grass where patients beat staff by seventeen wickets last summer.
The psychiatrist held to his promise to do the balloon dance in ward
round at Christmas (he did keep his red Y-fronts on).

Count
the knives out,
count them back.
We cooked apple pies,
with tang of Bramleys we'd
picked from the orchard, pastry
squidged fingertips, rolled out soft,
smooth, cut berry and leaf shapes; dress
proud golden crust, stardust
sugar
sprink l
e
d.

In art, you could
splatter despair on a canvas –
red, black and purple
fat bottles of paint;
put your work up on the walls in the hallways
to shout for you,
save your breath.

Institutionalisation? My arse!
They sold it for money,
spend less on us weaklings
more on the posh's executive homes.
They built a glass atrium over the entrance
where Bill used to piss on the roses
each morning
until they adjusted his meds.

They thought the towering fences
were there to keep us
shut in.
We knew they were there to save us
from them, who don't care,
who took our asylum away.

Tina

She trembles with the gale inside;
the push of tremors from her past
sinks her threadbare spine.
Ash-grey eyes reflect her pavement home
in front of once-was-Woollies.

She keeps the scars well-hidden,
pulls her long sleeves down
and grips them tight with bitten nails.
They'll give her a self-harm kit
in a bright green plastic bag,
so when she cuts another rung
at least it's with a clean blade
and a cosy dressing after.

You know she tells the truth
when she explains about her mother
and the beatings and the gang rapes
because that's not when she cries:
tears come when she sees you care.
Kindness bites her like a dog
she needs but cannot tame.

She asks for 50p and 50p
until she has enough for that night's room.
No more, no more than that
or you will make her cry.

Transgender We

Dog shit through your letterbox!
said wide-eyed Nurse Lucy,
all clipboard, concern,
and Unconditional Positive Regard,
That must have been terrible – terrible!
No wonder you're depressed.

Yes, shit, Jean nodded,
but I also had trouble with piss:
the first time I weed as a woman,
it went all over the floor...

then I found out;
you lean forward, don't you?

Oh! Let me think about that.
I've never thought about that before...
Well yes, yes I ***do*** *lean forward!*

Jean waited.

Pink

Here I am hoovering flamingos
again,
hoping
I'll shift heavy dust, reveal
astonishing pink,
satiny feathers,
boomerang beaks,
beady gold eyes that
know.

I'm not going to try standing
    on
    one
    leg
like a fool,
I'd fall over
again

and I'd want to keep falling
                                        out
of this monochrome monster.

I tore mistakes out of my exercise book.
My books became thinner and thinner.

Up on that bridge; oh, feeling the suck
of the river below!
Blue lights, high-viz yellow, burble and crackle of radios,
Come on luv, down now, I've got you....

Now the flamingos are dusty again.

Coconut shells

I.

I promised myself I would not look through the closed window
at the church tower clock again.
From this silent room I can see its blue tarnished face,
black iron hands and numerals.
I cannot hear the chunk and whirr of cogs and spindles.

When I hear twelve low, heavy chimes
I will attach my white veil to my silver headdress.

High overhead, an old sickly light gropes through the clouds.

Now I hear horses' hooves.
As a child, I made the sound with coconut shells.
Mother says, even though I'm too good for him, I must have a
carriage.

I promised myself I would not look through the closed window
at the church tower clock again,
so I find myself counting.

Mother says it takes precisely one second to say the word
'elephant'.

II.

She promised herself she would not look up at the white plastic
hospital canteen clock
again.
She sits, in her ice-white wedding dress, at a yellow-topped
table; the others all vacant,
apart from the one where the nurse sits, silently, watching.
The kitchen staff have gone home.
The cleaner sweeps the eggshell-white floor with a soft brush.
What's left of the evening sun glints on the bride's tiara,
shimmers down her pale blonde hair, then sinks away.

Her taffeta skirt engulfs the chair, fills the space beneath the
table.
Her veil tangles around a chair leg.
Her unthrown bouquet: yellow and ivory roses; amber
chrysanthemums;
daisies, shaped into a heart.
She picks the petals out one by one. They fall
on the yellow table and the white floor.
She promised herself she would not look up at the white plastic
hospital canteen clock
again
so she mutters, *elephant, elephant...'*

The cleaner's broom swishes.

Real Dereal

These are not the walls I painted.
This is not the blue sofa I bought.

No, I won't sit down.
I can feel this room stare
at the back of my neck.

It's true my heavy feet brought me,
as if they knew the way,
and it's true the Yale in my pocket
fits the lock in the grey front door.

But I've never been here before;
I can't stay.

If only I'd tied a red thread,
unspooled, held tight
to find my way home.

But where to attach it?
There was nowhere.

Concrete Moon

That 12-hour shift, the nurse walked 3.6 miles on the white non-slip floor, in low-heeled black leather lace-up shoes.
That 12-hour shift, the schizophrenic tugged his feet as if through treacle from his single room to the canteen and back three times. He wore blue flip-flops.

When it was time for medication, the nurse flustered over milligrams and millimoles.
When it was time for medication, the schizophrenic considered side effects.

The nurse wrote notes for 40 patients and two incident forms (in triplicate) with a black Bic biro.
The schizophrenic wrote *FUCK OFF* on his bedroom wall with the charcoal from four burnt matches.

At tea time, in the office, the nurse ate a sausage roll she had bought on the way to work from the One Stop.
At tea time, in the canteen, the schizophrenic ate macaroni cheese, surrounded by 39 other patients, also eating macaroni cheese.

The nurse looked up at the moon above the roof of the Arndale Centre on her way home, and thought it looked like concrete.
The schizophrenic looked up at the moon sitting just above the hospital incinerator chimney and couldn't remember whether it ever met up with the sun. He thought one day he would walk to the Planetarium in London because they would know, and because you can walk around London and no one notices you.

At bedtime, the nurse lay flat on her back on her small bed and turned off her bedside lamp.
At bedtime, the schizophrenic lay flat on his back on his plastic-covered hospital mattress and the ward strip lights blinked off.

The Sticky

It's shit-brown, snot-grey, tar-black,
spewing over the rim of their sack
as they hug it to their chest,
push open the door with their back,
shuffle across to the chair.

They sit, clutching it on their lap,
peeping over the top.
They can't put it down, not
yet, not yet.

They talk of that and this.
Sometimes they mention the sticky;
reach round the sack for the tissues.

Sometimes they empty it
into the air between us;
the sticky drops to the floor
in globules and puddles;
the sack exhales.
They leave the room, lighter.

But I have to clear up when they've gone
and the stench of the sticky clings;
the taste squats hefty on my stomach.
I vomit it up,
or at night, spit it out in my dreams.

Nightline

To me, he is in a silent movie,
white face, black eyelined eyes,
holding up a sign,
I can't go on!

I picture him
at the top of a towering tenement,
bass piano trembling,
honky-tonk,
ready to leap -
saved by two men in overalls
who carry a bulging mattress
along the grey pavement below.

I picture a steam train
coming closer, closer -
sputtering to a stop
before he can jump.

In my office, blue carpet, red phone,
I barter my rainbow ideas
for his black ones and white ones.

He has to agree, that life in Technicolor
holds more hope than
silence,
black and white signs,
and anyway, a whole house could collapse
and leave him simply brushing the plaster dust
from his shoulders.

Just before I click the phone down,
I hear white pills rattle
from a grey bottle.

I smile and dial
for a bright yellow ambulance.

In the End

After Langston Hughes

I've known people come in bellowing
in the grip of three policemen.
I've known people creep in,
silent, trembling.

I've known people cut their veins
and offer the blood.
I've known people set a match to their clothes
and watch the flames take them.

I've known people walk all day
and all night 'til there's no sole
in their shoes.
I've known people slide under the bed
and stay there.

I've known people bounce off the walls
after one night on the skunk.
I've known people crawl on the floor
after twenty years on the booze.

I've held them down,
picked them up,
filled them with drugs,
flushed drugs out of them.
I've walked them to a padded cell
and I've walked them, patched up,
with their bags to the Exit,

I've won and I've lost;
I've failed, and I've failed and I've failed;
but I've known mad,
I've known sane
and I've known people.

Acknowledgements & Thanks

'The Sticky' has previously appeared in: *Prole*, and in Louisa's *The Happy Bus* pamphlet, published 2017 by Picaroon Poetry. 'Nightline' was published as 'Emergency Duty' in *The Interpreter's House*, and a version of 'Accept the Diagnosis' was published by *Strange Poetry*.

Thanks are due to: Rob Campbell for his common sense; Stephen Daniels for his lack of it; Ira Lightman for clearing clutter, finding better patterns, and sharing his half of our poem; Helen Mcloughlin for her judgement; John O'Donoghue for being John O 'Donoghue; Tom Sastry for dog taming; Jackie Wills for the MOT and the Sussex Sticks for their love and honesty.

Louisa Campbell

Louisa Campbell was born into a strange religious sect. Her difficult childhood resulted in mental and physical health problems, which eventually led to her having to give up her beloved career in Mental Health Nursing. For seven years she was unable to write a word due to sedating medication, but having withdrawn from it in 2015, she started an Open University Creative Writing course and passed with Distinction. In her first year of writing she was shortlisted for the Bridport Prize, commended in the South Downs Poetry Festival Competition, and published in an array of online and print literary magazines. Her first pamphlet, The Happy Bus, was published by Picaroon Poetry in 2017. She lives in Kent with her husband, daughter, and two rescued Romanian street dogs.